VOLCANOES
AND EARTHQUAKES

D1304300

CONTENTS

INSIDE EARTH

Planet Earth is made up of three main layers: a thin covering called the crust, a layer inside the crust called the **mantle**, and a core in the center.

Cross-section of Earth

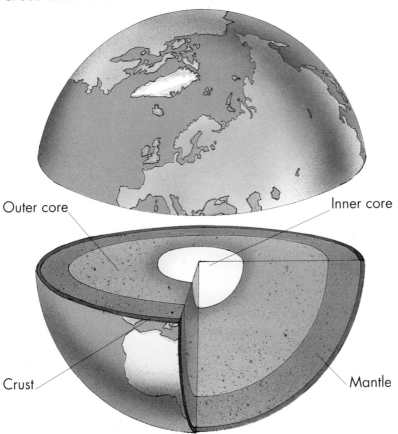

Outer core

Inner core

Crust

Mantle

Earth's Layers
The crust, made of solid rock, has two parts: the continental crust under the land and the oceanic crust under the sea.

The mantle is made from **magma**. The core has inner and outer parts. The outer core is entirely molten, while the inner core is completely solid.

EARTH'S PLATES

Earth's crust is made up of huge **plates**, which are pieces that fit together like an enormous jigsaw puzzle. These plates move constantly but at an extremely slow pace. They may push together, pull apart, or slide past or under each other. Earthquakes and volcanoes are most likely to occur at the edges of the plates. Mountains and trenches also form along the plate borders.

Moving Continents

The continents ride on the plates. When the plates move, the continents move, too. About 500 million years ago, most of the southern continents were part of a big landmass that scientists named Gondwanaland.

New Land

Gradually, the plates drifted and caused the landmass to break apart and come together again. About 325 million years ago, a new continent called Pangaea was formed.

Break Up of Pangaea

The large landmass of Pangaea began to break up, too. Over the past 175 million years, it split and re-split, eventually forming the continents as we know them today. The continents are still drifting. This makes Earth "alive," unlike the moon, which is considered "dead."

PLATES MOVING APART

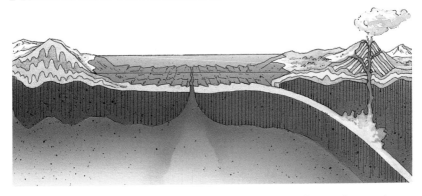

Currents of Magma
Molten rock from the mantle pushes up through cracks at plate borders in Earth's crust.

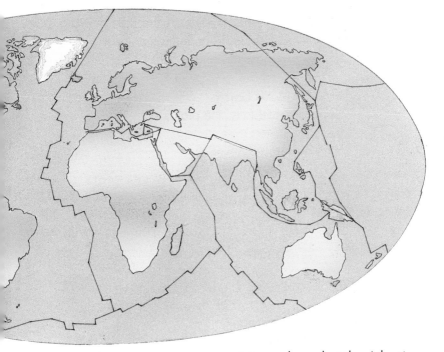

Plates and Water
Earth's plates move at about the same rate that human fingernails grow. Satellite pictures show that the Atlantic Ocean is growing wider while the Pacific Ocean is becoming narrower.

WHAT IS A VOLCANO?

A volcano is an opening in Earth's crust. A volcano is formed when magma gushes up from the mantle and breaks through a crack or weak spot in the crust. The magma lies in a **chamber** deep inside a volcano. Pressure builds up, forcing the magma to escape through a passageway called a **vent**. Once the magma reaches the surface it is called lava.

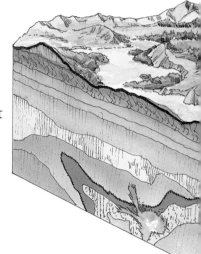

Volcanoes that erupt regularly are called **active**. Volcanoes that no longer erupt are **extinct**, or dead. **Dormant** volcanoes lie peacefully for centuries and then erupt suddenly.

Kinds of Volcanoes

Cinder Cones
The most violent eruptions produce thick lava that does not flow far. The lava cools to form the steep slopes of cinder cone volcanoes.

Basaltic
Basaltic or shield volcanoes are wide, low, and shaped like shields. They produce dark, runny lava and are often found on the ocean floor.

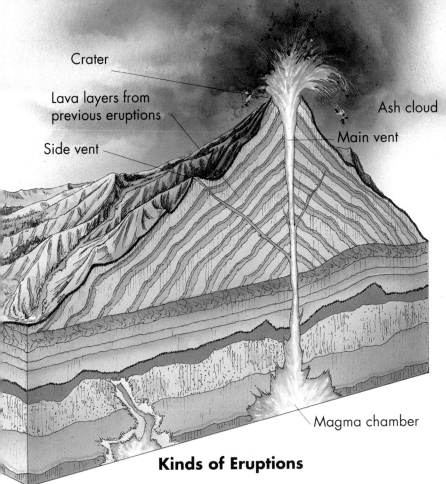

Crater

Lava layers from previous eruptions

Side vent

Ash cloud

Main vent

Magma chamber

Kinds of Eruptions

Hawaiian Hotspots Runny lava pours out from volcanoes with very wide bases.

Vesuvian Explosive eruptions from cone-shaped volcanoes are named for Mt. Vesuvius in Italy.

Strombolian Ash and **viscous** lava flow from volcanoes named for the island of Stromboli.

VOLCANOES UNDER THE SEA

More volcanoes occur under the sea than on land because the oceanic crust is thinner than the continental crust. Although most volcanoes occur along the edges of plates, some happen where the mantle gets hot enough to melt a hole in the thin crust above. These places are called hotspots. The islands of Hawaii, in the Pacific Ocean, were made by volcanoes forming over a hotspot and erupting under the sea.

Iceland: Land of Fire and Ice

Most underwater volcanoes cannot be seen, but sometimes layers of **pillow lava** build up into slopes. Eventually the volcanic slopes may grow high enough to emerge above the surface of the sea. This is how Iceland was formed.

Hawaii: A Chain of Volcanoes

As the plate under the Pacific moves, it carries away the active volcano that formed directly above the hotspot. This volcano becomes extinct. In this way, a chain of volcanic islands, like the Hawaiian islands, is created. An active volcano lies directly above the hotspot and extinct volcanoes lie beyond it.

Rift: where two plates move away from each other.

A New Island

In the 1960s, a new volcanic island gradually formed off the coast of Iceland. It took about four years for the pillow lava to pile up above sea level. The new island was named Surtsey after Surt, the Nordic god of fire.

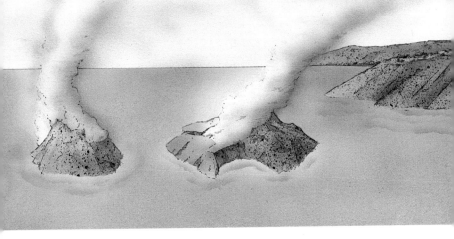

Mauna Kea

Most of this dormant volcano is hidden by the sea. Only its peak shows above the surface of the water. Mauna Kea will eventually become extinct as the Pacific plate moves away from the hotspot.

Trench: where two plates collide.

Hotspot

VOLCANOES AROUND THE WORLD

Many dramatic and destructive volcanoes have erupted throughout history. Today there are more than 800 active volcanoes on Earth. In the Pacific Ocean there are about 300. They are called the "Ring of Fire."

Blanket of Ash
When Mount St. Helens, in Washington State, erupted on May 18, 1980, a layer of hot ash covered the surrounding land.

Famous Eruptions
1. Santorini, Greece, 1628 B.C.
2. Vesuvius, Italy, A.D. 79
3. Mt. Fuji, Japan, 1707
4. Mayon, Philippines, 1814
5. Tamboro, Java, 1815
6. Krakatoa, Indonesia, 1883
7. Mt. Pelée, Martinique, 1902

Destroyed Civilization

In 1628 B.C. the volcano on the island of Santorini erupted, destroying an early civilization that flourished there.

Tidal Wave

In 1883, when the volcano on Krakatoa erupted, the island was almost destroyed. The land shook so violently that it caused a **tsunami**, a giant tidal wave.

Changed Climate

Mt. Pinatubo erupted in 1992. Gigantic clouds of dust and gases from the volcano polluted the air. These clouds drifted around the world, partially blocking the sun's heat.

3

9

14

4

6

5

Famous Eruptions

8. Stromboli, Italy, 1921
9. Mauna Loa, Hawaii, 1950
10. Surtsey, Iceland, 1963
11. Kilauea, Hawaii, 1971
12. Mt. St. Helens, Washington, 1980
13. Etna, Sicily, 1986
14. Mt. Pinatubo, Philippines, 1992

VOLCANOES ON OTHER PLANETS

Volcanoes do not happen only on Earth. The biggest volcano in the solar system is on Mars and is called Olympus Mons. Venus, too, has giant volcanoes, created by hotspots deep below the Venusian surface. Maxwell, the tallest volcano on Venus, is nearly one and a half miles higher than Mount Everest, which is Earth's highest mountain. Some volcanoes on Venus erupt continuously, pouring clouds of gas into the flame-colored sky.

Volcanoes on Io

The *Voyager* spacecraft found that Io, one of Jupiter's moons, has at least six volcanic vents. Plumes of sulphur gas from Io's volcanoes spurt hundreds of miles into space forming shapes that resemble huge umbrellas.

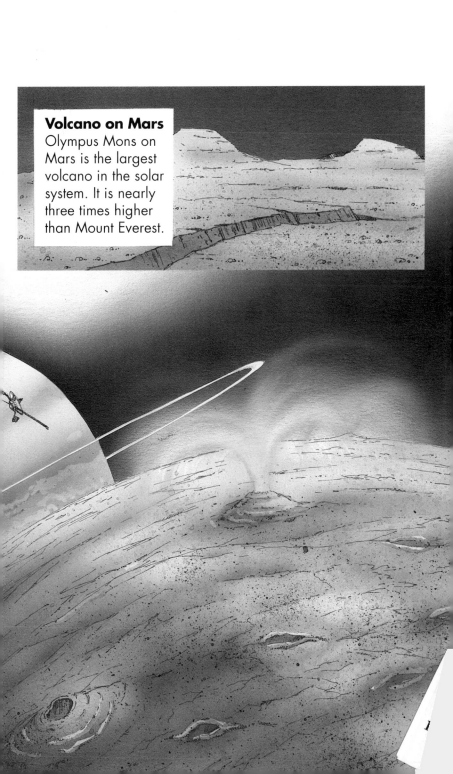

Volcano on Mars
Olympus Mons on Mars is the largest volcano in the solar system. It is nearly three times higher than Mount Everest.

LAVA

When magma from inside Earth pours out of volcanoes as lava, it cools and hardens, either on land or on the ocean floor. As it cools, the lava turns into a hard, dark rock called **basalt**. **Minerals** grow in the cooling lava, forming tiny crystals. You can see the crystals in basaltic rocks, especially if you use a magnifying glass.

Volcanologists

Studying and measuring volcanoes in action is the very exciting but dangerous work of **volcanologists**. They wear heatproof suits for protection. However, some volcanologists have been killed because of unpredictable eruptions.

Rivers of Rock

Some molten lava is like a red-hot river of rock, setting fire to everything in its path. Long after they harden, the lava and ash from volcanoes eventually break down and turn into a rich soil in which plants and trees thrive. Volcanic islands are usually lush and green with plenty of plant life.

POMPEII

Pompeii was a rich and beautiful Roman city built on the slope of Mount Vesuvius, a dormant volcano in Italy. Vesuvius had been dormant for so long that no one thought it would ever erupt again. Crops grew well in the volcanic soil, so the Romans built many villas, farms, and grand houses on the side of the volcano.

Vesuvius was not extinct as everyone thought. It seemed extinct because a lump of solid rock was blocking its central vent.

THE BURIED CITY OF POMPEII

The day Vesuvius erupted, life in Pompeii ended instantly. The volcano blasted hot ash high into the sky, blocking out the rays of the sun. Chunks of hot rock rained down and set the city on fire. Thousands of people suffocated from the poisonous gas of the volcano and were burned by the ashes that covered the city. Terrified people ran through the dark streets toward the sea, hoping to escape by boat.

Mount Vesuvius Erupts

On August 24, A.D. 79, Vesuvius erupted with terrible force. Hot poisonous gases gushed up, blasting the solid rock that had blocked the vent high into the air. Pompeii was soon buried under more than 20 feet of rock and ash.

The Buried City of Herculaneum
When Vesuvius erupted, steam rising from the volcano turned into water, mixed with the volcanic ash, and made a sticky mixture like hot, muddy cement. This rolled down one side of Vesuvius, completely burying the nearby town of Herculaneum.

POMPEII AND HERCULANEUM TODAY

Pompeii and Herculaneum lay
buried and forgotten for more
than 1,600 years. Soil, grass,
and vineyards covered the land.
The two lost Roman cities were
accidentally discovered by Austrian
soldiers in 1709. Excavations began

in 1738 at Herculaneum and in 1748 at Pompeii.
Scientists have been studying the ancient cities ever
since.

Pompeii
Centuries after the eruption
of Vesuvius, archaeologists
found the remains of
Pompeii perfectly preserved
under a layer of mud and
volcanic ash. Today, more
than half of the original city
has been uncovered.

Herculaneum
The modern-day town of
Resina was built on the site
where Herculaneum once
stood. This has hampered the
excavation process so that
only one-fourth of the ancient
city has been unearthed.

IGNEOUS ROCKS

Igneous rocks form when magma or lava cools. There are two types of igneous rocks: plutonic and volcanic. Plutonic rocks form when magma cools underground. This magma cools very slowly because the rocks above act as a blanket, trapping the magma's heat. Slow cooling allows the crystals to grow very large. Volcanic rocks form when lava, ejected from a volcano, cools above ground.

Pumice
Light, frothy pumice rock forms when lava cools quickly. Many little bubbles are trapped inside.

Basalt
Lava that cools slowly forms basalt, a dark volcanic rock with tiny crystals and few bubbles.

Granite
A plutonic rock with large crystals called granite forms when magma cools underground.

Hidden Features
When a very thin slice of rock is examined under a microscope, the **polarized** light reveals the shapes and colors of the crystals in the rock.

A Magnified Slice of Granite

Quartz

Feldspar

Mica

Pyroxene

Olivine

WHAT IS AN EARTHQUAKE?

An earthquake is a violent shaking of Earth's surface. Most earthquakes occur along **fault lines**, or large cracks in Earth's crust. The sudden tremors in these areas are caused by the build-up of tension whenever one of Earth's plates presses against another. The pressure sends shock waves through the ground. Every year, thousands of earthquakes are detected around the world. Minor quakes cause little or no damage. Major earthquakes can cause death and destruction.

Cross-section of an Earthquake

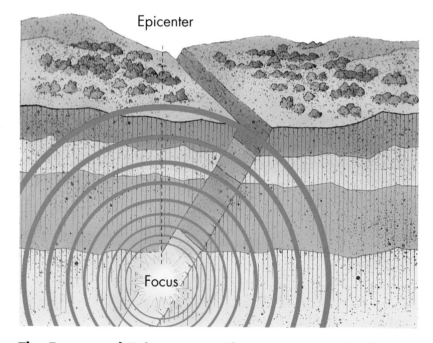

Epicenter

Focus

The Focus and Epicenter

The point within the earth where an earthquake originates is called the *focus*.

The *epicenter*, which suffers the most damage, is the point on the surface directly above the focus.

THE SAN ANDREAS FAULT

Many earthquakes happen around the edges of the plate that is under the Pacific Ocean. The most famous earthquake zone, the San Andreas Fault, is the most active fault line on Earth. The cities of San Francisco and Los Angeles in California are built near this fault line. Major earthquakes have struck both cities. An earthquake that hit Los Angeles on January 17, 1994, killed 61 people.

What To Do During an Earthquake

1. **Put out any fires**
   Fires can be more dangerous than the earthquake itself.
2. **Stay inside**
   Roof tiles, broken glass, or concrete blocks might be falling from buildings.
3. **Protect your head**
   Cover your head with a pillow or cushion. The safest place to crouch during an earthquake is inside a door frame.

The Earliest Earthquake Detector; China, A.D. 132

This early **seismograph**, designed by Chang Heng, is a jar with a heavy pendulum inside. Around the outside are four carved dragon heads, one for each direction: North, South, East, and West. Each dragon has a metal ball balanced in its mouth. Below each dragon is a frog. A quake causes the pendulum to swing, and knocks a ball from a dragon into a frog. This frog points toward the general location of the earthquake.

PREDICTING EARTHQUAKES

It is impossible to prevent earthquakes from happening, but scientists, called seismologists, can sometimes predict when and where a quake might occur. They use **laser beams** and other instruments to monitor active fault lines where Earth's plates are touching or sliding past one another.

Laser Beams

Seismologists use laser beams to identify rock movements before an earthquake.

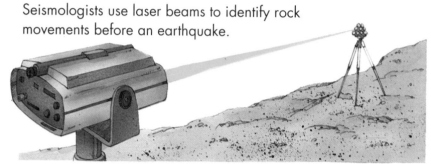

Sensitive Animals

Some animals can detect vibrations or changes in the ground, giving a warning signal before an earthquake happens.

Chinese Snakes
Prior to the earthquake in Haicheng, China, in 1975, snakes left their burrows.

Japanese Catfish
Before the earthquake in Tokyo, Japan, in 1923, catfish jumped out of their ponds.

MEASURING EARTHQUAKES

The size of an earthquake depends on the size of the fault line and how much the plates slip. The Richter Scale measures the force of each earthquake, giving it a score from 1.5 and 8.5. Most earthquakes score only about 2, but an earthquake that measures 8 could flatten a city. The Mercalli Scale ranks earthquakes from level I to level XII, according to the amount of shaking and damage they cause.

A Richter Scale recording of an earthquake

The Mercalli Scale

SEISMIC WAVES

The release of tension from the movement of Earth's plates causes vibrations that pass through the ground in the form of waves. At the site of an earthquake the shaking lasts only seconds, or at most, a few minutes. But the shock waves, or **seismic waves**, generated at the focus continue to move rapidly outward, spanning the globe in about 20 minutes. Primary, or P-waves, are fast. Secondary, or S-waves, are slower. Both pass *through* the earth. Long, or L-waves, travel along Earth's surface, causing damage near the epicenter.

QUAKEPROOF BUILDINGS

The extent of earthquake damage depends on where the earthquake strikes, the number of people living in the area, and the types of buildings found there. Although nothing can be done to prevent earthquakes, careful planning can reduce the amount of damage they cause. Many buildings in areas likely to have earthquakes are specially designed so that they will sway instead of collapse. Steel cables, or "jackets," are used to strengthen the buildings. Special foundations help absorb ground movement and reduce shaking.

FAMOUS EARTHQUAKES

LISBON, PORTUGAL 1755

Tens of thousands of people died in the Lisbon earthquake of 1755. Some people were killed by falling buildings. Many more were killed when huge fires broke out afterward, destroying what was left of the city.

TOKYO, JAPAN 1923

Tokyo, the capital of Japan, is built on a fault line. In 1923, while families were cooking their midday meal, an unpredicted earthquake struck. Low wooden houses collapsed without hurting many people. But a whirlwind of fire followed the earthquake, killing thousands.

TANGSHAN, CHINA 1976

On July 28, 1976, one of the greatest natural disasters in history occurred in Tangshan, China. The city had been built over a gigantic coal mine, with many tunnels under the city. When the earthquake hit, all the tunnels collapsed. Tangshan was destroyed, and almost 650,000 people were killed.

ARMENIA 1988

In 1988, an earthquake struck the small country of Armenia. An international rescue effort helped the victims. Specially trained dogs and infrared cameras which can detect body heat were used to find people trapped under the rubble of fallen buildings.

TSUNAMIS

Earthquakes and volcanoes under the ocean can sometimes cause a giant tidal wave called a tsunami. A tsunami can be more than 100 feet tall and can destroy everything in its path. This occurs in and around the Pacific Ocean. A warning system has been set up in this area to alert people about an oncoming tsunami. A tsunami travels at speeds of up to 500 miles per hour, which is faster than a jet airplane.

Formation of a Tsunami

Drop a stone in a pond and watch the ripples. The effect is similar to the pattern created by a seismic wave underground and a seismic ocean wave or tsunami. As the ocean floor rises near the coast, tsunami waves become taller, reaching enormous heights.

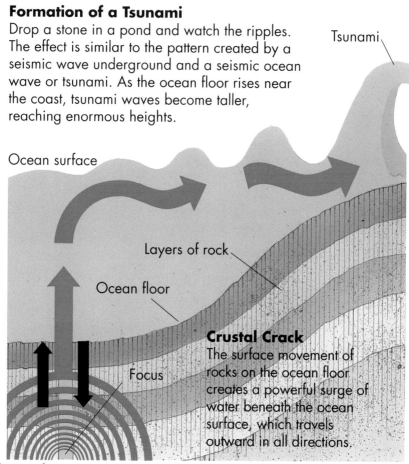

Tsunami

Ocean surface

Layers of rock

Ocean floor

Crustal Crack
The surface movement of rocks on the ocean floor creates a powerful surge of water beneath the ocean surface, which travels outward in all directions.

Focus

HOT ROCKS

Volcanoes and earthquakes sometimes leave small holes in the ground called **fumaroles**. Gases from inside Earth escape through these fumeroles. Hot volcanic rocks can heat water under the ground. The water becomes so hot that it turns into steam and gushes up out of the ground in a boiling fountain called a **geyser**. Sometimes the heated water bubbles through cracks in the ground, forming hot springs.

Macaque Monkeys
Monkeys keep warm by bathing in the hot springs in Honshu, Japan.

AMAZING VOLCANO & EARTHQUAKE FACTS

• **Tsunami** The highest tsunami ever recorded occured off the coast of southern Japan in April, 1971. The wave created a great wall of water almost 300 feet high.

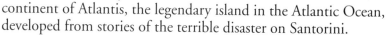

• **Atlantis** In 1628 B.C. the volcanic island of Thera (now called Santorini), in Greece, erupted. All life on the island was completely destroyed. People believe that the story of the lost continent of Atlantis, the legendary island in the Atlantic Ocean, developed from stories of the terrible disaster on Santorini.

• **Krakatoa** When this volcano on the Indonesian island of Krakatoa erupted in 1883, the noise made by the explosion was so loud that it was heard by people living in Australia, almost 5,000 miles away! It was the loudest noise ever recorded.

• **Geysers** Old Faithful, one of the most predictable geysers, is in Yellowstone National Park, Wyoming. Eruptions used to occur every 65 minutes, but are now every 75 minutes due to recent earthquakes. The tallest geyser ever recorded is the Waimangu Geyser, near Rotorua, New Zealand. In 1903, it spouted up to a height of 1,500 feet!

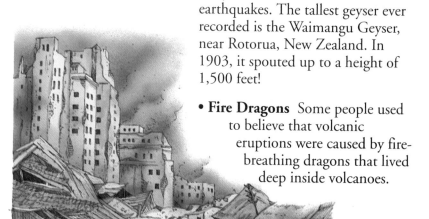

• **Fire Dragons** Some people used to believe that volcanic eruptions were caused by fire-breathing dragons that lived deep inside volcanoes.

GLOSSARY

Active volcano A volcano that has erupted at least once in the past 10,000 years.

Basalt A dark, hard volcanic rock that is composed of tiny crystals.

Chamber The area deep within a volcano where hot, molten rock is found.

Dormant volcano A volcano that has not erupted in the past 10,000 years.

Extinct volcano A volcano that is thought to be dead.

Fault lines Cracks in Earth's surface. They may form valleys, mountains, or earthquakes.

Fumarole A small hole in the ground through which steam and other gases are released.

Geyser A spring of hot water, heated underground that spurts up as steam at regular intervals, like a fountain.

Granite Rock cooled deep within the earth and made of large crystals.

Laser beam A straight line of light that can be used to identify rock movement.

Lava The very hot, melted rock ejected from a volcano.

Magma Molten rock inside the earth, ejected as lava.

Mantle The area between Earth's crust and outer core.

Mineral A crystal that makes up rocks. A mineral is formed naturally in the earth.

Pillow lava Pattern of lava produced by underwater volcanoes.

Plates The parts of the outer layer of Earth that move very slowly. There are eight major, and some minor, plates.

Polarize To transmit light waves vibrating in one direction.

Seismic wave A wave caused by an earthquake.

Seismograph An instrument that measures ground movement.

Tsunami A tidal wave caused by an earthquake or volcanic eruption under the ocean.

Vent The passageway up and out of a volcano through which magma erupts.

Viscous lava Lava that does not flow freely.

Volcanologist A scientist who studies and measures volcanic activity on Earth.

INDEX *(Entries in **bold** refer to an illustration)*